Ryan Quinn Flanagan

Gangbangs and Other Mass Rallies

Copyright © 2017 by Ryan Quinn Flanagan

Layout: Pski's Porch
Cover design: Pski's Porch

All rights reserved. No part of this book may be reproduced in any form by any electronic or mechanical means including photocopying, recording, or information storage and retrieval without permission in writing from the author.

ISBN-13: 978-0-9988476-3-4
ISBN-10: 0998847631

for more books, visit Pski's Porch:
www.pskisporch.com

Printed in U.S.A

"When one burns one's bridges, what a very nice fire it makes"
— *Dylan Thomas*

Contents

Spit Bucket 1
It came down from the top 2
Theo and the Little Yellow House 3
A Little Love for the Punks 4
Milking Your Prostate is Not like Milking a Cow 5
Distance Runners Miss the Point 7
Gangbangs and Other Mass Rallies 8
Eyes & Ears 9
Feeding the Machine 10
Hoover 12
Dykes on Bikes 13
An Evening of Drug Trafficking 14
Burial Wrongs 16
Truck Stop 17
Geminis Suck 18
Picasso Couldn't Paint Worth a Shit 19
Pinched 20
I Started Thinking about Jesus 21
Bloodlust and Chicken Wings 23
Vermin Kept as Pets 25
in the Landlord's Monthly 25
Cage 25
I'm No Angel 26
Sweet Science 27
Dummy Companies, like Incorporating the 28
Mentally Retarded 28
Drinking Games Where Only the Bottle Wins .. 29
Successful Business Trend 31
The Crucifixion Racket 33
Give 35

Dried Soup and Water Damage	36
Be Kind to Atheists	38
A Very Simple Question	39
There is a Reason She Buys Unsalted Butter	40
Kuklinski	41
Attrition Monger	42
The Spent Condiments	44
of the Nothing	44
Generation	44
Water Damage is Just Liquid Revenge	47
Good Teeth	48
The Ghost of Your Ideas Left Behind	49
Nervous	51
White Rhino	52
Live Ins	55
The Return of Max	57
You Could Do Worse than Lawn Furniture	59
Korean Karaoke	60
The Starry Night	62
The Interrogator	63
Beds that are also Couches	64
so the Efficiency Expert can Sleep	64
at Night	64
Enlisted Man	66
Pick & Choose News	67
A New Pair Each Day	68
Usury	69
Three Song Set	70
Invest in the Future, and Even Nostradamus Laughs	72
Bedbugs	74
Pavement is Hard	75
A Box of 100 Letter Size File Folders	76

Robots	78
Continental Breakfast	79
Party Politics	80
Handshakes Are a Gateway Salutation	82
Martha, Martha, Martha!	83
Body Condom	85
Seeing is Believing	86
Making Things Official	87
Gangs	89
City, City	90
Bootleg Bonanza	92
Writing Couples	93
Another Ice Bucket	94
Hostages	95
$900 Phone	96
Heading Downtown	98
She keeps	99
Pissing Blood	100
A Bull Named Hokum	101
24 Floors of Kierkegaard	103
The Crimes They Are A-Changin'	104
It's a Wonderful Life (the poem)	105
Fender Bender	106
Concerts	107
Skater Shop	109
Flop	110
Winter Sports Out of Season	111
Je me souviens	112
Aggressive Sales Tactics	113
like Swallowing a Shotgun	113
for Breakfast	113
Boat Yard	116

7 Hour Sitting	117
Hustle	118
War Years	119
Talking Shop	121
Half a Million Tiny Dead Mayans Behind Me	122
Systems Analyst	123
Two Sides of a Different Coin	124
Bayou Betty Finds Her Place in the Throaty	125
Stomach Acid Amalgam	125
The Receptionist	126
Partial Eclipse	127
Bundle Up	128
Falling Out of Bed	129
like the Last Days of	129
Saigon	129
Besties	130
Split Personalities, in a Physical Sense	131
27lbs in 4 Weeks	132
A Woman of Race	133
Art House	134
Sofia	136
Basement Apartment	138
Zebra Mussels	139
Ramen	140
Punctured Lungs & Cryostasis	142
Breasts Are Not a Sexual Thing	143
Dish Hogs	144
Lose the War, Win the Fight	145
Big Winner	146
She Had a Nice Smile	147
True Story	149
Weak Play	150

Lunar Eclipse	151
The Queen's Speech	152
Sashimi Thin	153
Full Uniform	154
The Real Thing	155
Tiny Marathon Runners with Flush	156
Numbered Bellybuttons	156
Bathroom Break	158
Fluency Test	159
Life	160
Holdout	162
PTSD	163
Sporting Goods	164
Vampires with Hate for Horse Blinders	165
The Artist and The General	166
Did you hear the one…	168
Expiration Date	169
Consumption	170
Pickled Requiem	171
Centenarian	172
Late Night Feedings	174
Exit Strategy	176
Swimmers without Goggles	177
Hell, with a Broken Radio	178
On Fighting	180
Long Lines at the Grocers	181
so Cars can be Loaded full as	181
Sniper's Rifles	181
Major Depressive Disorder	186
Work Clothes	187

Spit Bucket

She spit into his mouth
and he was pretty sure he had hepatitis
or worse.

The torn fishnets, the broken
fidgety gibberish.

A needle still hanging out of her arm
from past indiscretions.

All because his drunk friend had
made a comment about deep sea fishing.

And now he was down on his knees
choking over the curbside.

Beside a rusted brown sewer grate
with a used condom draped
over it.

It came down from the top

It came down from the top
like an avalanche,
the factory was to close down
and relocate to South America,
jobs would be outsourced
and cut incrementally over a fourteen month period
beginning with all temp workers
and part-timers and making its way through
the ranks of the full-timers until there
was no one left.

Then the whole area would be fenced off
and dynamite would be employed.

A controlled explosion
like losing your temper,
but never hitting
your wife.

Theo and the Little Yellow House

Vincent did not want to be a burden
to his brother and his new family.

The apartment in Paris was not big enough
for them all.

In Arles
the Little Yellow House was perfect,
the studio of the south.

Nibbling at turpentine soaked bristles
and painting sunflowers to spruce up the guestroom
as he waited for Gauguin to arrive
from Brittany.

And when the thing went sour,
handing Gauguin that newspaper clipping
that read:
THE MURDERER FLED
before rushing off into the darkness
where both he and brother Theo
would be before too long.

A Little Love for the Punks

The great thing about a GG Allin show
was not the questionable musicianship
or the feces thrown at the crowd,
but that it forced you to react.

Like a car crash
when your life depends
on it.

Milking Your Prostate is Not like Milking a Cow

I drop my pants
sit over the bowl
and it comes spilling out
of me.

There is a great release of pressure
and a strange absence of smell.

I look down between my legs
to make sure what I think should
be there is there.

It is.
Liquid squid ink black.
The red wine from the
night before.

And that deep rushing, like everyone making for the only
exit
during a fire at a nightclub has caused me
to milk my prostate.

To cum without any thought of a woman.
A single thick growing globule hanging there
off the end of my flaccid cock.

When I wipe it away, it doesn't want to go.
Some of it sticks to the tip, and a little more comes out.
Milking your prostate is not like milking a cow.

Mostly, it is just a lot of dabbing,

and a little bewilderment.

My pants still down around my ankles
like prison shackles from a former
life.

Distance Runners Miss the Point

It is best
to say a lot
with very
little.

Most say little
with very little,
or even worse,
with a lot.

The more words
you need,
the more you have
failed.

Everything
simple and poignant
and direct.

Gangbangs and Other Mass Rallies

There is nothing wrong
with large numbers
of people
working towards a singular
purpose
unless of course,

you are that singular
purpose.

And you find that –
with arched back
and ass
in the air –
you have
their undivided
attention.

Eyes & Ears

She said
the government was
watching her

listening in on all her
conversations

and I told her
to not live with
so many
cats,

that
all those eyes
and ears
on her
had made her
paranoid,

especially around

feeding
time.

Feeding the Machine

That giant green monster
of Scarborough

belting out miseries
so the screeching soprano
could sleep in

that giant binding machine
of sleepless terror

and human components
through the punch clock door
in shifts

I have worked them all –
there are no winners

and I fed the machine
and everyone else fed the machine
and the supervisors would turn up
the speed to make quota

and it was impossible to keep up
but we all tried
feeding more and more of ourselves
away with each shift, month,
year…

bags under the eyes for a pittance
the muling back shot
straight survivalism

eventually I would place the pages in the feeder
unevenly so it would jam
and the machine operator would cuss me out
and the floor super would keep a close eye

but there was a momentary lapse
as they removed the jam
before starting up the machine
again.

Hoover

I was a weird kid.
I used to keep files on all the neighbours.
Study their daily movements and interactions.
Watch their many infidelities, nervous ticks, shopping habits,
the way they treated their animals and parked their cars etc.
Noting any sudden departures from the norm.
Then I would write them down and file it away.
In a drawer full of file folders arranged by address.
And I did this for years.
My obsessive-compulsive behaviour always with me.
And the heavy brown leather double strap of my father's
high powered binoculars rubbing against
the sides of my neck.

I also set booby traps for Santa.

Determined to catch him
in the act.

Dykes on Bikes

These two lesbians
used to ride past our place
along the Queensway
a few times a month
on matching pink choppers

with a banner that read:
Dykes on Bikes

except that one had a sidecar
with a small dog in it
that wore goggles

and seemed to get excited
about everything

and when they stopped at the lights
they would blow exhaust at all
the cars behind them

and their ride by would be
the highlight of our day

as we wheeled our tiny pushcart
of dirty work clothes
in a single black
garbage bag

to the coin laundry

down the
street.

An Evening of Drug Trafficking

I once had this bone thin junkie
grind up against me
at the Silver Star Club
in downtown Barrie
before asking if I could get her
any weed.

I pointed over to my friends
and mentioned it was my birthday
and that perhaps she would like to
do a little more for appearances
since they had paid for
a dance,

but this one was so out of it
she went straight to business
and I told her to give me her number
and I would check with my
connections

when my one and only connection
was why I was already high,
not caring in the least if she straddled
the ribbed crown of every headstrong unicorn
in an eight block radius
or did damn near anything
at all.

But I guess word got out backstage
that I had connections
so the next three song set

stole my hat and rubbed it against her pussy
in a way steam cleaning can never fix
and went backstage with it
so that I had to go talk to all
of them.

Within ten minutes
they thought I was a major drug trafficker
and I had all of their numbers.

I may have played it up after a while,
but can you blame me?

You couldn't have that many naked women
in a single room
if you had put clothing on
the endangered species list.

And I was just turning eighteen.
Which made all the rest of it so unbelievably
ludicrous.

My girl asking me how the boys' night out went
a few nights later.

I told her it was uneventful
and that I was defrosting a microwavable
pizza.

Burial Wrongs

He asked me to stick around
after a couple drinks
because there was once a fondness
of person there

but now
he stuck needles in his arm
and passed out with lit cigarettes
burning through his fingers.

And the girls that came around
all had death in their eyes.

The same way you look at a tombstone
and see nothing.

And when they put him in the ground
it was like watching them plant potatoes.

And you can call me an asshole for that,
but you have never been there.

I was the only one.
In ceremonial black.
No friends or family.

Not even the tombstone girls
would brave the cemetery.

Truck Stop

The truck stop was littered with sloppy meatloaf faces.

Lot lizards and dish hogs and a communal copy of Penthouse in the Men's crapper.

The toilets clogged like never coming up for air.

The mirrors all smashed out for their
jagged forgetfulness.

And there was an old shoeshine machine in the corner
which you could feed quarters into,
but it didn't work.

The out of order sign just weathered faces
that had forgotten how to smile.

Geminis Suck

One black girl working the towel kiosk
by the pool at the Luxor
tells another black girl working with her
that she is a Gemini.
Some skinny white kid working with them
says: Geminis suck!
I'm a Gemini too, says the second black girl.
I know, answers the skinny white kid,
that is why they suck.
Both black girls are playfully angry.
They seem to like the white boy.
And he wants one or both of them.
Like pulling at the pigtails of the girls back in grade school
so they can pretend to be terse with you.

It is Spring. Even in the desert.
The birds aren't the only ones having
at it.

Picasso Couldn't Paint Worth a Shit

You are sailing along fine
through the slipstream
until you get that first
one.

Who spits on the tip of your dick
and spreads it around with her hand
before going to town.

Some of it still attached to her face
as she separates, looks up into your skull
and says something crazy like:
Picasso Couldn't Paint Worth a Shit!

And it is not only crazy because Picasso could paint
missing children off milk cartons in his sleep,
but because you realize it is some clumsy drunken
metaphor
that she wants you to paint her face
when you cum.

And this is the moment you realize
you might have met a woman
who has enjoyed more porn then you
and old Pablo put together.

A woman who fingers her own ass
while checking the mail.

Pinched

Mitch and Carl had raided a delivery truck
a few weeks back.

As it sat at the back loading dock
of some box store in the east end of the city
while the driver was inside with
the paperwork.

And they started selling cigarette cartons for scratch.
And it wasn't long before someone snitched
to escape their own predicament.

And Mitch and Carl were pinched.
For both the robbery and selling to an undercover.
And the race was on.
Mitch gave up Carl almost as fast as Carl
gave up Mitch,
but they already had everything they needed anyways
so the signed confessions were just icing
on the cake.

Who smoked all those cigarettes?
I'm guessing some croupy cough cops
with a river of nicotine
for lungs.

Evidence goes missing every day.
Just like children.

I Started Thinking about Jesus

and how the first one to anything
gets crucified

and how the checkered flag
of race car driving
was a trap,

that bees knew to circle the hive
on principle
rather than necessity;

about how she was pulled
out of school
all those years
ago

and they said it was because
the family had moved cities,
but everyone knew she was
pregnant,

and no one knew who the father was,
but our Social Studies teacher
took a leave of absence and never
came back

and school dances
became closely
monitored

in a way they had
not been before

by people
who had not been
there before.

Bloodlust and Chicken Wings

The bus route
is not the paper route
is not the trade
route

slimy black grasshoppers
jumping out of their own
legs

the field I am standing in
is not the field where Van Gogh
finally did it

it is tilled, full of corn
somewhere in the American
Midwest

could be an Indian burial ground
or just a bunch of anthills,
no one can be sure of these things

and the shopping here is fantastic
as long as you have no money
and even less taste

the cars along the interstate rush by
like people walking faster to avoid
the muttering drunk at the bus stop
looking to unload his daily
sermon

and I close my eyes
hold my hands out palms down
feel a faint dry wind along
the underside

forgetting all about bloodlust
and chicken wings

the slow wet fury of arsenic
poisoning

have you gargled the slippery water slide
of modern cinema?

wondered why silent treatment Chaplin
ever let clumsy loudmouth death
ever get the best
of him?

Napoleon invading Europe
under the false assumption that
HE was Europe, amateur mistake,

the hive will always protect the Queen
and never the honey

and when I leave this field
I will take a part of it
with me

and park my car in such a way
that the ruling classes will know
I mean business.

Vermin Kept as Pets in the Landlord's Monthly Cage

Barbarians
sluices beyond the flood
sheets of cooked foil underfoot
the rat high – vermin kept as pets
in the landlord's monthly cage;
I pull out all my nose hairs by hand these days
because tweezers are an excuse,
no different than sandbags piled high
as condominiums, man bun coffee baristas
with the key to the bathroom
and little else.

The good times are good
so the bad times can be
a little less.

Such things seem fair
to an enterprising
mind.

I'm No Angel

have you seen
that movie?

I had never known a woman
like that.

Mae West
was a straight up
killer.

Like a spitting cobra
no wicker Madras market
could ever
hold.

Not even sexual,
and that is where the art came in.
She was second to no one.
Almost like she was not even another person
on set.

I am sure the movie houses never
intended that.

There was a very careful formula
back then
just as there is now.

But Mae West was the first woman
to escape prison.

The first woman I was afraid to fuck.
The ultimate compliment.

Sweet Science

Couples argue as much as they have sex,
often much more,
and I had a ride home from work
but preferred to walk
even on rainy days, letting the wet of the land
soak through and bite me,
and there was this bar along the way
which served recycled beer
and allowed you to die in peace
in dark corners
with spotty gum stuck walls,
and when I got home she was waiting
arms crossed at the door to meet me
demanding to know where I had been
even though she knew,
so that I could accuse her of sitting on her ass
doing nothing all day
and she could scream at me for being drunk
which I was.

Dummy Companies, like Incorporating the Mentally Retarded

Sores fester.
There was an uncle on popular television
named Fester.

More guidance systems than counselors –
almost a million-to-one.

The abacus will not lie unless you pay it to lie,
that is the spark plug behind everything.

Plausible deniability at a price.

Offshore accounts and offshore drilling.
Dummy companies, like incorporating the
mentally retarded.

And I put on my old lady's nylons.
Hop down the hallway like the frontrunner
in a potato sack race to the death.

The lipstick smears still heavy
so that I smack my gums together
like banging a dust broom
against a wall.

Drinking Games Where Only the Bottle Wins

Pull a book off the shelf,
is it still there?

The glue of the spine holding things together.

That musty reek of dog-eared pages
flipped though like old
playing cards.

Drinking games
where only the bottle
wins.

A family of raccoons
in the back shed
entering the housing market
free of charge.

And shoots of grass
under clumsy lawnmower
slippers.

A woman who paints her bathroom black,
but will have nothing to do
with abolition.

I love this life
for no other reason
than its treachery.

Cabs that refuse you in the streets

even though you are well dressed
and a fare

and
waving.

Successful Business Trend

You have nothing, she mocked,
no job or place or anything.

That's not true, I countered,
I have you.

She said I didn't have her
and I reminded her of what had
just happened on her very
own bed.

The sheets still sweat through with effort.
A traumatized cat named Sir Fluffiltons
with its face to the wall.

You think you're the only one?
she chided
trying to hurt me.

No, I answered.

WHAT DO YOU MEAN NO?

Many grocery stores stay open 24 hours now,
I said,
it is useless to fight a successful
business trend.

She was so angry she starting gathering up her belongings
to leave her own place.

Don't forget your jewellery box, I said,
some of that could be valuable if
it were real.

And I'd like to say we had angry makeup sex
after that,
but she was just angry.

It wasn't like in the pages of Penthouse
at all.

And when I found myself working at a carwash
a few weeks later
there was a rag in my hand
and a rich man with crazy white teeth
telling me to get
all the spots.

Not knowing what to say to him
I started wiping.

The Crucifixion Racket

I read somewhere
that they are still crucifying people
in some areas of the world

and I got to thinking that Jesus
or his estate
will be suing for royalties
if he ever existed

there is some serious money
to be made in the crucifixion
racket

think of all the worshippers, churches,
revivals, death row born agains,
fire and brimstone fallout shelters,
spread his word group hug bumper stickers,
wooden wall hangings in
his likeness…

T-shirt sales alone are enough
to fill Rome's coffers ten thousand
times over.

I can imagine whole marketing teams
sitting around
trying to repackage the
rising.

Everyone loves a comeback.
Ali after five years away from

the game.

The son
of a lowly carpenter
rising above his caste
in the latest pair of Nikes

just as you can

for $149,
before tax.

Give

To meet anything
with such a complete
and unbridled
violence

that it folds up
like a flower
in reverse
bloom

before
you,

that is how
I approach
anything,

even the pulling
of an elastic
band

Dried Soup and Water Damage

besieged
as though you should have a fort to defend
or a trench or bunker or opinion
or something

and I peel an orange around the middle
trying not to break the peel until
I have completed the circumference,
reverse Saturn, I tell myself,
idiotic and short of breath

my kitchen is dated like me,
a backsplash of dried soup
and water damage

an old fridge you have to bump into just right
to stop it from humming

and I would go outside, but there is nothing
out there for me, not today;

my clothes begin to smell like me
so that we become largely
inseparable

the way you stop having to lean in
to smell under your arms
because the stench has come
to you

and the wet under my arms

leaves stains in the couch fabric

I decide that I will shower tomorrow
because I have to go outside,
sustain myself in this way…

Something to fortify me
from the cracks in this faltering
city.

Be Kind to Atheists

All the secrets
that you're keeping

never realizing
the thick yellow continuance
of their ugly wet
reality

and don't ask garage shop unbelievers
about the wheel,
you will not like their answer,

it will be filled with air
and devoid of anything you wish
to hear

divergence is hardly a crime,
freeway off ramps do it regularly

be kind to atheists,
not too kind or they will take
advantage

as any

but understanding
is a good thing
even if no one really believes
in it.

A Very Simple Question

What do you think you are going to tell me
that I do not already know?

That is my one and only question.
After that, I will not speak for three months.
Call it a hunger strike if you wish, I will
be eating.

My yellow privacy curtain
pulled over so D.H. Lawrence
can tell me about women
in love.

There is a Reason She Buys Unsalted Butter

They meet in a back stairwell in the fashion district.
Outside of the general purview of the better business bureau.
Something for the needle in exchange for something for the pocket.
Sweaty, desperate, tax-free…

Adam Smith hunting for veins.
The wealth of nations, street level.

Winos smashing bottles like fine china
in piss dark alleys.

A purse full of mouthwash
to dilute the sodium
intake.

Kuklinski

You never know who you are dealing with,
that is the problem.

Gandhi or Gonorrhea?
What lies behind door number three?

So everyone should be on their best behaviour,
but they are not.

Breaking into cars, filling closets full of mothballs.
Catcalling the woman on the arm of another man.
Urinating on the sides of midnight houses that may or may not
be awake.

That is the chance you take.
Like those young Georgia fellas all those years ago,
bumping a car with New Jersey plates
off the road for fun.

Not realizing it was the most successful hitman
in mob history
with a fully loaded cannon
in the trunk.

When they found the bodies, there were five of them.
All lined up like stiff blue fence posts
that should have known better.

Attrition Monger

The average human being can go a long time
without sex, trust me.

Or any human contact really.
You start to count things that would never count
normally:

the transfer of spittle during cold season,
the exchange of monies in the checkout line,
pressing the button for the light to change
on top of all the other fingers that came before…

And when someone finally does come along,
they are usually just as desperate and despicable
and deprived as you.

Your air becomes their air.
Duplicate keys cut for ceremony.

It is nice to sit down and talk more than anything else.
But then they talk too much, and you start wanting your
privacy back.
Like their problems just magnify your problems
and perhaps everyone is better off alone.

But you stay together longer than you should
because there is always that fear.

Taking long walks alone in the park
and extra hours at work.

Anything to avoid that conversation before you are on your own again.

The Spent Condiments of the Nothing Generation

showing promise
in a promising land

peering behind refrigerators
for the grease answers

food courts with ridiculous red trays

the spent condiments
of the nothing
generation

ridges along the fingertips
so distant mountains can be imagined
sure as hay fever

tiny packets
exsanguinated of all sugar life
and smeared across long
plaster corners

walls even,
like they have in China
and once had in
Berlin,

walls to prop up a klutzy
accident-prone sky

destitution and inertia
just things you find in a shoebox
under the bed

coughing away dust layers
as your sausage fingers mind-fiddle
through stringy afterbirth

wiping things on the side of your pants
that are not your pants

the hands over buttons
like a reader of Braille

careful to avoid separation
or meaning

inconsequential as a tree gnat

my laboured breathing
no longer unionized

the dues became too much
just as anything does
with time

musicality and spray foam
in equal measure

lusting after words like some
silly prepubescent thought-ninny
on his way to drivel land

constructing office towers of sloppy sex

for the window cleaner's
measured eye

everything habitual, redundant,
and self-harming

a mezzanine cocktail
before your flight

and the muted Ahab wails
of a once promising
land

where no one finds anyone else

not even in a house
of mirrors.

Water Damage is Just Liquid Revenge

You look up at the ceiling
and find something other than
clouds.

Water damage is just liquid revenge
best I can figure it.

We've done so much to the oceans and lakes
and rivers and creeks and streams
that you have to expect some
push back.

I'm surprised there is not more,
but then I am surprised by
many things.

There is a fine line between idiot savant
and genius
and I am nowhere
near it.

I once tried to hold my pants up
with a broken fan belt
to make my car
jealous.

It didn't work.

Good Teeth

I had this one
with good teeth
tell me that all my
isolation did not make
me an artist, it made
me crazy,
and with time I can see
that she was right
and that everything
I am is wrong
and all the others
like me
licking the baseboard
heater for forensics
and eating oatmeal
out of the same bowl
with a solid green rim
for three decades
amount to less than
pocket change
in a world without
pockets.

The Ghost of Your Ideas Left Behind

The nail gun drove the stud deep into the wall
and I thought about my parents
on birthdays and anniversaries.

How I could hear them through the walls:
moaning, screaming, grunting
like animals.

All those years of my youth.
Covering my ears with a pillow
to drown out the noise.

And the way they would have friends over
at Christmas
and drink too much and fall into the baseboard heater
after pretending to be Santa,
laughing on their way
up to bed.

And the Jamaican transplant who dropped a saw
over my wrist at the end of the workday
many years later.

I still have the scar.

When people see you as nothing,
you become that for a while.

The ghost of your ideas left behind.

Then the self-hate becomes a little less.

But the fear of the alarm clock remains.

Its little red numbers burned into your skull.
Even when you are out of work.

The fear never leaves you,
and still the hate.

Nervous

I can tell she is nervous
because her nipples are threatening
to hack through her shirt
like the child labour of the
burgeoning palm oil
market

sporting child soldier scars
and machetes large
as the sun.

And she sits across from me,
sips at her drink like slowly opening a suspected
mail bomb in careful increments.

If this is love, I don't want it.
She makes me feel like a predator
in my own home.

If this is lust, I hardly have the time
or inclination.

A man grows old fast.
Almost always in the presence
of others.

White Rhino

He sat at the bar
because funerals should be surrounded
by wood.

Thinking about the woman
he met in the elevator
every day for three years,
and how she hated
his existence

like driving the white rhino
into extinction
with each forced
smile,

standing with her back against the lift
arms crossed

ogling the slow yellow beeping countdown
of the numbers to the lobby

until she could be rid of him
again,

and the way the man in the lobby
was always happy to greet you

like he wanted to shoot himself in the face,
but could not get a gun

and the landlord was a stickler

for gentrification

and soon
everyone had stainless steel
appliances

and sat in tapas bars
buying up olives for the price of caviar
to music that would put you
into a coma

if you were not already
in one

which is why he found himself
forced out

and living in a neighbourhood
that still had actual
bars

where no one was considerate
and everything reeked
of urine

and the felt on the only pool table
was torn apart as though a horny wolf pack
had recently mated upon it

and his head grew dizzy from drunkenness
and lack of sleep and food

so that he convinced himself that
the woman in the elevator

all those years ago

secretly had a thing
for him

and got angry at you for that
just like they did in the
playground,

that his poverty
and sagging beer gut below the belt
were oddly charming

and that she was tired of King Crab legs
and men who owned yachts

nudging the slumped over body
on the stool beside him
to explain his new found
findings

as the bartender with braces at forty-five
made a gesture of distance
with his hands,
so that he was back
in the elevator
again

watching her wind the cords
of her starving red Walkman
around unusually slender
fingers.

Live Ins

We moved into the new place
and there was someone already
living there.

Mice in the walls
that made their way down through
the vent above the stove
and had themselves quite the party.

Trouncing through the cornmeal
eating through spice packets
leaving droppings everywhere.

And under the sink
where the gettings were not nearly
as good.

We had to throw everything out
when we could hardly
afford to.

But we set up traps
and flushed enough bodies
to grace the cover of Serial Murder Monthly
a couple times over

and soon the place
was ours.

And we stayed there a year
and 7 months,

really made a home
of it.

If anyone knocked,
we answered.

The Return of Max

My horrible neighbour's cat Max kept running away
for a few days at a time
each time she didn't close the door
quick enough,
and she would be standing out in the yard
every few days after that
yelling his name with that wonderful
cheese grater voice,

the one that screeched to the heavens
and shouted obscenities at a constant parade
of men at all hours,

probably why Max needed his little vacations,

and one night both him and the other cat escaped together,
it was an all-out jailbreak, a one-time offer
and when she called, the other cat went back
like a chump, but Max did not.

And many months passed.
During the harsh Canadian winter.
Best I could figure it, Max had either
weaseled his way into the home
of some crazy old cat lady to be hand fed
cans of albacore tuna forever,
or he died.

The neighbour was out calling for him
for about a week before she gave up.

I guess she thought the same thing.

But today Max came back.
It is spring and the snow is gone
and he is sitting by my door
looking most full and healthy
and impassive.

He still has his blue collar on,
but it might be a new
one.

The neighbour must have seen him
because she is screeching for him
to come.

And he keeps looking over at her
as if to say:
look bitch, I don't need your shit!

It is in the way he looks with obvious derision,
then turns and walks away
again.

You Could Do Worse than Lawn Furniture

The thing I like about lawn furniture
is that it never talks politics.

It is goofy and ridiculous beyond belief,
but I know a world of people like that.

And they talk about politics day and night.
It hurts my head in a way the common headache
could only dream of.

And another thing about lawn furniture:
you can sit on its face and it never complains,
sometimes for many hours
until your ass grows
numb.

When people do that to other people,
someone always complains.

Usually someone else, not even directly involved,
who claims that act itself
IS political.

Korean Karaoke

We are at this bar in the south end
so the drunk girls in our group
can express themselves
after a night out.

Hanging off each other
in groups of five or more,
two to a microphone,
shrieking out the hits of
yesteryear.

Drinks in hand.
Murdering the Top 40.

Their boyfriends in the front row all spurring them on
as though a record deal is just around
the corner.

Anything to get laid.
The young male mind is no puzzle.

And there I am.
In my early 20s.
Chatting up the old Korean matron
who turns the light on over the billiard tables
and keeps count.

She tells me what it was like before the war,
why they came over.

Her English is quite good.

I am pretty sure she is lying,
but agree to the need for a 38th
parallel.

The old timer in the kitchen
slamming his knife down
like the final word.

The Starry Night

was a one
off.

Most people don't
realize that.

They see it hung in galleries now
and think that is how Van Gogh
painted.

Not knowing that Gauguin had challenged him.
To paint something surreal and he came up
with this.

And now
it is roped off
in galleries
around the
world.

Because one artist asked another
to step outside his comfort
zone.

The Interrogator

finally lost it:
*do you not think
there will just be another
one of you lazy gangbanging idiots
sweating it out in that very same
seat tomorrow,
telling me the same sorry tale
like I have never heard that one
before?*

Hey Thatcher,
he bangs on the door,
*I got C-rock in here today,
who we got lined up for tomorrow,
D-rock?*

*E, F, G-rock
so I have to drive out
and tell the families?*

Are you kidding me,
a life sentence at eighteen?

(no response)

*Cuff this asshole
and take him over to
lockup.*

Beds that are also Couches so the Efficiency Expert can Sleep at Night

The water falls over your hands
like liquid spastics
into a sink basin beaten out
of the general bathroom nightmare
with lead pipes

and someone starts making homemade postcards
and someone else stands in front of mirrors
sucking it in, imaging the clumsy suction
of angled vacuum love

beds that are also couches
so the efficiency expert can sleep
at night

the factory is productivity
in human form,
hands after hands as though cloning
a massage parlour ten million times over
and setting it loose on the fed pablum
of bald-headed parking meters

and the paper towel from the roll
is a child leaving home

my hands sufficiently dry to make purchases
and gang signs in equal measure

the fly done up

and the street walker
as well

coin laundry malcontents
tumbling dry cycle out
of hell

and I have worked enough of the convenience racket
to know there is little convenience
in anything…

Time is wrong.
All the clocks have lied.

Enlisted Man

He said
he was the illest man
and since I didn't know
what that meant

or thought I may have heard him wrong

I congratulated him
on joining the armed
forces

and asked him
if women really did
have a thing
for a man

in
uniform.

Pick & Choose News

The news broadcaster picks the stories
they think are newsworthy
and the personalities read from teleprompters
like reading your order back off a menu
with nothing on it
and the television audience sits at home
muting the stories they don't want to see or hear
and watching the ones they do
so that everything is self-affirming
and no one ever need think see hear feel
anything new
so that the ratings go up with favourability
and the personalities and broadcaster
keep doing exactly what they
are doing.

A New Pair Each Day

Panties
beside the toilet
in the
bathroom

a new pair
each day

piled up with rotting
compost exactness

so that you know your woman's
lining is falling out

like the stuffed innards
of a winter coat

and not to touch her
for a while…

you have been together
long enough
that the system
is in place

I can't remember when it started,
but every man knows
what it means

like farting in an elevator
and knowing that you have all
shared something.

Usury

Apparently the banks
and the credit card people
are immune.

What is a crime for some
pads the bottom line
of others.

I guess you need to make things official
to have it count.

Have all your paperwork in order.
Rubber stamp that shit.

Then you can call it "the economy,"
and not a crime.

Hell,
call it whatever
you want.

All the right people get their envelopes
at the first of each month.

I was never good with numbers,
but it seems many other
people are.

The law standing behind them
like a long line at the grocery
store.

Three Song Set

I was young
so the strip joints
were exciting.

Where else would a woman
give herself a full gynecological exam
two feet from your face,
then stick a pink glow in the dark dildo
up her ass
to the popular sounds
of the day?

I was happy.
The world was hardly mine,
but there were shelters.

Like mice in the walls
you never know are there.

What was sad
was the many old timers
that would sit in the back
with sunglasses.

Old white Europeans.
Alone at the table.

There since noon
to avoid the $5
cover.

Hustled by the dream.
Squeezed out of their pensions
by competing interests:

the schoolgirl
black leather
the mother with child
in need of sugar
daddy
all that…

And the girls always referred to them as lifers.
Like their ghosts would still be there
when they were gone.

And I usually never felt too good
after that.

Even when I was drunk.

Imaging the ghosts of all those old dead men
standing in on private dances
behind the glass
because they were ancient history
now

and no one could see them
with their cold dead hands
down their pants.

Invest in the Future, and Even Nostradamus Laughs

Tell me that is not the ultimate hustle.
Money up front for something you can't see.

That may or may not happen
and you wouldn't know either way.

But your continued support is most appreciated.
I bet it is.

All the way to the bank.

Ever wonder why forty whining strays
end up on your front porch
each night?

Word has got out.
You are an easy mark.

Like pickpockets
bumping into bank
machines.

A brighter future, they promise,
always a brighter future…

Tomorrow
is the vomit in the back
of the throat
of today.

But all you see is unicorns.

Notice how they replace the word money
with support
and leave you feeling good,
that is paramount.

Like watching a crayon picture
of a space capsule get hung on the fridge
and wondering what the universe
would look like if it ever got
there.

Bedbugs

I could tell they were bedbugs
as soon as she lifted her leg,
that pattern of three bites all in a row
and she let out a horrible scream,
covered her mouth like someone who had
been blood-suckled out of sleep.

And her belongings were scattered across the floor.
Like the remains of a Vietnamese village
after the latest carpet bombing.

And I told her to shower
and leave her stuff right where
it was

and back out of the room
like a car out

of the
driveway.

Pavement is Hard

He had not wanted to be on the rooftops
of buildings,
but a gambling debt had lead him there,
hung upside down over the ledge
failing to see the beauty of the many
gothic style gargoyles

as the goons that had him by the legs
reminded him that pavement
is hard

and the loose change fell out
of his pockets
onto the honking ravenous
streets below.

A Box of 100 Letter Size File Folders

I strip down to my underwear
because it is Sunday.

A man should be relaxed on the weekend.
The stores close early.

And I pick the elastic bands out of the
undersides of my undies.

Snap them between my fists
as though I am big into manual
strangulation.

Getting the chair,
more as a protest against seating arrangements
than any desire for state execution.

And the books on my shelves all read themselves.
Breaking the spine in a self-masturbatory way.
Tolstoy, so large that he has to be cut out of his house.
The Russian peasantry picking through his
meager belongings.

And I head downtown
to buy a box of 100 letter size
file folders.

And death on the installment plan.

The back cover torn away
so that the used bookstore guy

gives me a break on the
sticker price.

I love that musty hospital death smell.
Multiple floors your bloated sausage fingers
can rifle through for days.

The titles of the dead and dying
jumping out at you like the pages of
numbered acrobats.

The goodies pierced
and perhaps a solid plot
too.

It is good to stroll the avenues.
To walk with people behind you,
imagining all sorts of knifings.

And the air you breathe just came from space.
Fills your lungs with blocks of alien Lego.

And you relax because it is the weekend.
Slow to a crawl like plagiarising the garden snail.

Paint many pictures in acrylic
with your face
as they do in the bloody
wild.

Robots

She has all these robots now.

There is the one she holds in her hand
to take many doctored pictures of herself,
and the one on the floor that maps the layout
as it goes around the house cleaning the floor
and carpets every Saturday at 10:30pm.

And the one strapped to her wrist
that tells her how far she has walked
and when it is time to go to bed.

The one on the floor is most unsettling.
It seems willful and strangely intelligent.
Stopping just before the stairs so it doesn't fall.
I keep waiting for it to start fashioning tools
or master the art of language.

And I'm pretty sure we don't like each other.
The same way two kids on a playground will just eye
each other at a distance.

I don't say anything bad about it
because I am pretty sure it is listening.
Even when it is just sitting in the corner.

For her part, she loves all her new robots.
Has taken to giving them names like children.
And like children, they will grow up to hate her.
Except they are an army of robots,
which doesn't seem good.

Continental Breakfast

The continental shelf
held the continental breakfast,
but we were all too small
and inconsequential to
ever reach
it

with our makeup bags
and angry makeup
sex

and rear-view mirrors
like going back
in time

on a
budget.

Party Politics

There appear to be three separate groups:
the women in the main room, the men in the kitchen,
and the peripheries mingling about like spiders by the walls.

The women are loud and always smiling
and sharing gossip over white wine.

The men are more discreet.
Huddled like an American football team
discussing a play.
They are in the kitchen because the fridge
is in the kitchen, and that is where the beer is housed
that is not already in their hand
or down their gullet.

And the men and the women make eye contact
every so often, smile, then go back to talking
amongst themselves.

The peripheries are an unpopular afterthought,
really just there to fill out the ranks
so the hosts can impress upon the others
their popularity through numbers.

I am a periphery, an acquaintance from work
that is here for the beer.
I do not even really like the host that much.
His wife is a chatty bulimic with a steel wool cunt.

But the beer is cold and free
and their walls are filled with many
pictures to look at.

There is also someone responsible for the music.
Both volume and content.
Almost always one of the most trusted women
of the group.

And the food is laid out like slabs at the mortuary
and picked over by packs of hungry vultures
with disposable plates in their hands.

Aside from the restroom, this is the only time
the groups will break off and disperse.
Their plates and glasses refilled, everything
congeals back together just as it were before.
And the hours go by like this.
Many shoes piled by the door.

The peripheries will leave first
because they are not really there.

Followed by single men who have struck out,
then pairings of men and women from least-
to-closest friends.

Then, only the stragglers remain.
Drunk with nowhere else to go.
They must be pushed out the door
just as you turn away a door-to-door
salesman.

The front light turned out.
Cleanup always waits until morning.

The fresh gossip begins right
away.

Handshakes Are a Gateway Salutation

to be avoided at
all costs

a ruse of the Russians
or the Chinese –
let's say the Chinese
for effect…

Disarming
just like Oppenheimer
before the bomb.

Getting you to smile
when your face should
know better.

Martha, Martha, Martha!

Martha had been a chubby bespectacled kid in high school
and said I made her feel that way
all over again.

I could not fathom why she was with me,
but we paid rent together and had a landlord that hated
us both.

He used to slide notes under the door
so he didn't have to talk to us.

His wife had left him.
I always wondered if she had just slid a note
under the door and never came back
and this is how this whole note writing
business began.

But Martha was skinny now.
She starved herself thin and blamed me
for that.

I wasn't an angel either,
but at least I was not like her parents.
They had recently come back into her life
because she was no longer fat.
I knew better then to point that out,
she would have just blamed me for that
as well.

Proximity is a bitch.
Spend the majority of your days less than three feet

from each other's face, and do not be surprised
if some plates get broken.

The resentment on both sides built up
like a brand new condominium complex.

Stealing the sky from migrating birds.

And when we split, it was ugly.
Like watching a child run over by a car
bleed out in the street through
little people clothes.

Or acid thrown into the faces
of arranged marriage.
Ugly like that.

And I got my own place.
There are drawbacks to that too,
but it was alright.

A basement bachelor along Trapor
that flooded with each
heavy rain.

And I never saw Martha again.
And nobody slid stupid little notes
under my door, although I still looked
for them at all hours even though
it made no sense
at all.

Body Condom

He was the best defense lawyer in the country.
Wore his mistress' silk panties to trial.
Almost all of his clients were guilty,
so he wouldn't hear of it.
Just the details: who, where, when,
what, how…
Big on search and seizure.
Civil rights abuses.
Wrapping himself in the law like a body condom
he could use against itself.
Knowing he did not have to prove innocence
as much as he had to instill doubt.
The best defense is a questionable offence.
And to always minimize everything.
Make culpability look like pocket change
you almost forgot about.
Inconsequential as carpet dust.
To tell a story.
Provide a strong working narrative that the jury
could understand.
Simple enough to have done it yourself
without even realizing,
but sordid enough in legal complexities
that even the law itself would be confused.
And that is the real aim.
To use the letter of the law against itself.
To poke holes in everything so that
nothing ever leaves the ground.

Seeing is Believing

Go exist in a decommissioned
missile silo in rural Kansas
for top dollar

for all I
care

I have seen the whole
of the human race
live horribly

and continue
in the worst
of ways

betraying the ones
they love
so convincingly

the moon could land
on itself

and call
foul.

Making Things Official

We are ring shopping in a mall in North Bay.
More to make things legal than out of any momentary whim.
We have been together 20 years.
Longer than some countries.

Basically,
we want to write out wills
and have them be legally binding
so that neither family can interfere
with our wishes when the time comes,
simple as that.

And we've settled on very affordable bands.
Decided to elope in April
over four days in Vegas
at the Luxor
with a discount from American
Airlines.

I just hope we don't get a room that looks onto
the ass of the sphinx.

I've been warned about them on Trip Advisor.

If I wanted to see Sphinx ass
I would travel all the way to dusty
Egypt.

Drink too much
and get into an argument

with the locals
about how Ramses the second
was the Justin Timberlake
of the ancient
world.

Gangs

The kids all join gangs now.

They used to join sporting teams
which I guess were a
sort of gang.

They provided uniforms
and a sense of belonging
and an adversary that
needed to be
overcome.

I hated team sports.
I had to do everything myself
and it was never enough.

Which is much the same reason
why I would never join a gang.

But the kids these days are all in gangs.
You can't tell one from the other.

And they have their own signals.
As though even the street lights are lacking
in some way.

City, City

The city is so busy,
everyone in a hurry to get somewhere,
but there is nowhere to go
so I do not understand the rush,
I watch them step on the backs on each other's shoes
and curse one another before rushing off again,
others fight with umbrellas in the rain
car horns met with car horns like some sad
imitation game.

And everyone is medicated now.
And not just coffee.
Over the counter remedies for the zombie
on the go.

And the buildings blot out the sky.
They are meant to be glorious and imposing,
but they are just stupid.
Pigeons flying into the plate-glass of a false sky
with serial arson regularity.

I walk into stores now when I don't need anything.
I often do not even know what store.
I am just trying to avoid the crowds.
But the inside is as bad as the outside.
The same way surgery sounds like a good idea
until they start cutting.

And I know I sound like some 300 year old curmudgeon,
but I am a 38 year old man.
Relatively young according to the national average.

But the bustle of this city wears on me, makes me haggard before my time.

Lines form on my face
as though waiting impatiently
for their turn at the cash.

Bootleg Bonanza

The Marquis de Sade
selling out in the back alleys
of Paris.

Papa Hemingway running copies
of Ulysses into the states.

Metallica's No Life 'Til Leather
rousing the Frisco underground
into a frenzy.

Everything
should be like that,
but almost nothing

ever
is.

Writing Couples

I have nothing to do with writing couples
if I can avoid it.

Isn't one sorry narcissist enough?

Putting two together just seems like
locking two angry drunks inside a shoebox
and letting them wail on
each other.

I feel bad for the shoe box.
And anyone who may ever read
the result.

The same goes for fine artists.
Those monsters have turpentine
to throw at one another.

Same sex, opposite sex,
no sex…

It doesn't seem to matter.

There are plenty of daily massacres the world over
for you to enjoy without putting two writers
together.

Can you just imagine the sheer unadulterated carnage
of the editing phase?

My missus never reads the stuff.
We have been together almost
twenty years.

Another Ice Bucket

Standing beside the ice machine
another ice bucket
with swim googles for eyes
shuffles up beside me
digs down into the hepatitis
and says: I half expect a body in there
each time I reach down.

He reeks of chlorine and low resolution child porn.
Business lunches on the expense card.
I imagine his body in there.
Chopped up finely as Japanese sushi
under a high end New York
knife.

Returning to the room
I tell the woman walking out
of the shower
with a towel on her head
that they were out
of ice.

She makes a face as though she may not
believe me.

Tells me to pour two anyway,
and I oblige.

Hostages

There is no such thing as hostages.

There are people you want back,
and people you don't.

And a government will secretly pay
for those they desire,
and not pay for the rest.

But as for this whole hostage business,
I remain thoroughly unconvinced.

Anyone who wants to be taken
will walk into a local pawnshop
or bank or trust the taxman
before they hop a plane
and fly 13 hours nonstop
to end up in an orange
jumpsuit.

It is simply a question of ease.
What can be done in under an hour
will always be done.

We are lazy that way.

Watching the kettle boil
because even the water
is taking too long.

$900 Phone

Puddles becomes lakes
in extreme climates,
and we let the cars go by
before we walk around
because they are metal
and we are not
and broken bones take
recovery time.

We are in North Bay for the first time.
The missus doing a bridging program
from the university here,
but that is our
only link.

And within twenty minutes
of entering the mall
the missus has a new
$900 phone.

Somehow I do not feel taken
although the salesgirl was very good.
At first I thought we would get the hipster douchebag
leaning against the glass
and there would be problems,
but we got the salesgirl who seemed to know
what she was talking about.

And she made things easy.
Like they must have been in the absence
of humanity.

And now we are in the food court.
Snapping our first picture before seeing a live band
downtown in a few hours.

A band we have seen many times in our youth,
but the years catch up with everyone.

Her brand new $900 phone
trying to edit some of the years
out of this.

Heading Downtown

We were heading downtown
after visiting my grandmother in that
old red brick second floor apartment along Blake Street,
my aunt Marilyn keeping my cousin Shauna and I
on different sides and making us
hold her hand

and I remember skipping over the working ants
careful to avoid the cracks in the sidewalk
and feeling so incredibly happy
under the sun

for no other reason

then my aunt was my aunt
and my cousin was my cousin
and anything could happen,
but it never did.

She keeps

her balled up
silver "S" necklace
beside my toothbrush
as though she is trying
to remind me

of all we've been through
and all we've lost

knowing I will see it
each time I brush my
teeth

and even though I realize
she is pinching a page
straight from those remote viewing
psychological warfare heavies
I don't really care,

if she feels the need
then so be it,
but rescued dogs aren't
this loyal.

Pissing Blood

no man
wants to go
there

like
one of those
old Roman fountains
with bronze cherub wee wees
giving up the
farm

so you can snap some pictures
of the old world
and lose your face in summer
gelato

while I stand over the
morning bowl
and wonder why anyone
would ever invent
such an uncomfortable word

as
urethra.

A Bull Named Hokum

To go to sleep
alone
is hardly the worst
thing in the
world.

There could be
the absence of pillows
or no sleep
at all.

Watching the bull red numbers
of alarm clock Pamplona
rush through the
streets,

a bull named Hokum
goring the last of your
tired sanity

while patio stone onlookers
sip at wine

and get the most
out of resident
murder

trying to name olives
like strange children
you abort

in a pinch

because they are
mistakes

you never imagined

that want names
and laugh at the funnies
just like you.

24 Floors of Kierkegaard

The trees will not stop barking
so why yell at the dog?

Many colourful obscenities
that I have not heard
in some time.

From the mouth of a woman
who thinks no one else is listening,
but can go right into victim mode
instantaneously.

But the dog knows better
and I know better.

It is a secret we all share.

So the laughing gas world
can have its atom bomb fun
from the 24th floor of nihilism
that never bothered with
an elevator.

The Crimes They Are A-Changin'

This giant fat kid spit on me
in the playground once
and it made me so angry and disgusted
that I broke his nose and knocked his front teeth out
and made him choke on many handfuls
of sand

and somehow we became friends
after that
inviting each other to
our birthdays

for many years

which seems like a rather curious thing
to do all these years later

when the volume of the neighbour's tv
can have you banging on the walls at all hours,
wishing another Stalinist
purge.

It's a Wonderful Life (the poem)

The baby shit itself
and wailed
for the better part of three days
before it was discovered
crawling across its dead mother
with a needle in her arm.

On a single cum stained mattress on the floor.
Like gravity has more of a hold
over others.

Shifting cockroaches for walls.
Mouse droppings in the
pablum.

A window open finally
for the smell.

Fender Bender

She seemed panicked
after the crash
as though breathing into an oxygen mask
of straight terror

and I thought of the spotty dreams
of crouched jaguars through the mangroves

of pheromones in the glove compartment
beside the flashlight full of
launch codes

and she kept pushing the oxygen away
from her face
even though they said it would help

as low motility air bags
that had neglected to go off
sat in traffic beside us

and the trigger fingers
of amateur hunters
failed another safety
test.

Concerts

I don't like concerts
because concerts are filled
with people.

I enjoy the bands
and their music,
but never the
people.

And we are very modern now,
buy our tickets over the computer
months in advance,
so who you end up beside
is a blind crap shoot.

But it is always some drunk asshole
with his girl spilling her drinks
all over you.

One time
I had this guy make his leg dance so emphatically
to each song that both our legs
danced together.

Even when I was not dancing.
I guess we shared a moment.

The missus still laughs about that one.
The guy beside her sat still as
a bag of soil.

Pirating the whole show
on his iPhone
so he could upload it
to the interlink
hours later.

Skater Shop

Standing out front
this skater shop
in the mall

I feel a lot differently
than I did before

it may be the years

twenty of them
if we are counting

while skinny jean virgins
dye their hair yellow
in numbers
thinking that will make
a difference

as the missus tries on
plus size bras
to hold her

knockers
in.

Flop

After fourth street he felt desperate,
backed into a corner like a rabid animal
of shrinking returns,
and when the river dropped
he went all in,
betting everything on nothing
a straight bluff
standing up for effect

and the house was not rattled:
everything on nothing, they laughed,
so you want to get married?

I am married, he confessed.
Then what are you doing here?
the house asked.

A married man should get fucked at home
in the presence of his wife
and kids.

And when they went all in,
he knew everything
was lost.

The wife and kids back to her mother's
and his clothes on the front lawn
like dressing the grass
for church.

Winter Sports Out of Season

The mirror breaks
and my fist may or may not
have had something to do
with it.

There is blood everywhere.
I wear towels over my feet
and slide across the tile.

As though I am ice skating indoors.
Winter sports out of season.

And the door begins knocking
so I assume there are fornicating mice
having at it.

Then a voice that asks if everything
is alright
and since everything is better than alright
I reassure that voice

by sliding a few crumpled
bloody bills under
the door

and waiting for the authorities
to arrive.

Je me souviens

She loved that I could speak French
even though I couldn't
speak French.

I knew what many of the words meant
on sight,
and just rolled my Rs when
I could.

Women love a man who can roll his Rs.
It is all about the tongue.
And other dextrous things that tongue
may be able to do.

It took me a long time to figure this out.
I come to everything slowly.

But I was really popular back in sixth grade
French class.

The girls began to take a real interest in me
after that.

Aggressive Sales Tactics like Swallowing a Shotgun for Breakfast

You are in the mall.
The gaping runny nerve centre.
This is how space travel would be
if you had swallowed up all your oxygen
in a single thirsty binge
and started pushing buttons
at random.

The jeweller's kiosk under lock and key.

The food court
a collection of ugly unwanted dolls
with their faces kicked in
one after the other.

A prison lineup where everyone squeals
for muddy pig freedom.

Oily bike chains left in the street.

And the illumination is false,
but the sales tactics
are real.

No one legally allowed to hump you
like a silverback gorilla in the firm mating sense,
but there are loopholes.

Aggressive sales tactics

like swallowing a shotgun
for breakfast.

Bits of cranium peeled off showroom cars
that sell for sticker price.

And you find yourself in public bathrooms.
Beside shoplifters stuffing a day's haul
down their pants and hoping no one
would ever want to go there.

Throwing the hangers to the floor
and leaving.

One after the other.

As you look to the empty roll
beside you
and make other plans.

Tapping the hypothalamus
in Morse code
for hints.

And the people on their phones
have become their phones.

You jump out of the way
to avoid contact.

Some kid in faded jeans
shoving a phone plan into your face
faster than you can duck away.

Down the alleys of your youth.
The dollar store full of crying children
named Elijah.

That have shit themselves
in a way you have not
in years.

Boat Yard

One of the best jobs I had
was a one day gig
on this boat yard out in
Innisfil Township.

Cleaning boats I could never own
in three lifetimes.

And smoking so much weed with the two regular guys
that I stood over the hose and watched the sparkling water
for many hours.

And these guys did nothing.
There was no boss around.
They couldn't even stand or talk.
They just sat there with their sunhats
pulled down over their faces
giggling every so often.

Unfortunately for me, it was just a one day gig.
My fifteen year old self drinking from the hose
when I got hot.

While the little silver radio belted out tunes
that had never seemed
so good.

7 Hour Sitting

The missus
is getting her half sleeve
done in the Soo.

By an artist no one knows about,
but they should.

And it is a 7 hour sitting
so they have a VCR set up
and a collection of movies.

When I am hungry
I walk the two blocks south
toward the US border.

To the Station Mall
where I order some New York Fries
and try to find a seat far away
from other human beings.

Within moments of sitting down
a mother sits at the next seat over
with its child looking at me
as it picks its nose and
eats it.

I get up and move.
To one of those swivel seats
that look away from
the commons.

Wondering why the hell they still have bookstores
when no one reads.

Hustle

I can understand
the braggarts
and the low key
gents as
well.

No one
has the answer
so we keep
throwing rocks
at the moon.

Like those old rock n' roll stations
out of the south
in the 50s.

Hoping someone
out there is
listening.

War Years

*I'm glad we didn't have to live through the war years
like our grandparents, she says,
my grandmother used to draw on all the girls' legs
because they needed the nylon for the war effort.*

*But there are wars going on, I say,
many of them all over the world every day.*

*I mean the ones that mattered, she says,
the world wars.*

She is half-watching the television on mute.
Some show about luxury cruise ships and all the problems
the rich can have getting from one place
to another.

I am picking my oily beard hair from my face,
looking at it, then tossing it to the floor.

We are under a water warning again.
Boiling everything until we get the green light.

A dragonfly slams headfirst into the screen
of the back sliding door, steadies itself,
then flies off.

There are divots in the walls
that would cry foul if you ever called
them imperfections.

Can you imagine the lawsuits?

Someone somewhere angry with you
because they are really just angry
with themselves.

And how their lives have turned out.
And now you have caught their attention.
If they can just kill you, that will somehow make them more.
The logic is not there, but when has it ever been?

Billboards large as the sun
promising zero down.

While fleas jump from the carpet
in a game of low income
hopscotch.

Talking Shop

We worked the loading dock
at this box store in the west end of the city.

I was the receiver
and he was my forklift
driver.

And we had it down.
A real good system.
Five trucks in seven hours,
plus breaks.

During the holiday
high season.

Then we would head over to the peeler joint
before they started charging cover.

And talk shop.
Nurse our $7 beers.

Watching the girls who had slept all night
hug the pole with their ass cheeks
like others will embrace a lover.

Half a Million Tiny Dead Mayans Behind Me

The flowerpots were all grooved
and overturned
so that it looked like miniature Mayan temples
with the soil removed.

All in a row
lining the walk up to
the house.

And when I rang the doorbell
her father answered.

And his words said he was happy to finally meet me,
but his eyes said something else.

And her mother was curled up like the family cat
with a book, yelling up to her only offspring
that her date had arrived.

As my mother sat by the curb
in a running old powder blue rust box
you had to stick a screwdriver in the choke
to start.

And the house was twice as big as ours.
And that shouldn't mean anything but it does.

With half a million tiny dead Mayans behind me,
all wanting to sacrifice my heart
for more rain.

Systems Analyst

Respiratory: shortness of breath
Nervous: seizing, anxiety, and depression
Lymphatic: white blood cells on the rampage
Muscular: pulled, malformed, and osteoporosis
Reproductive: non-existent
Exocrine: excessive sweating and white hair
Endocrine: testosterone imbalance
Digestive: where to begin
Renal: pissing blood
Cardiovascular: insufficient

Two Sides of a Different Coin

I remember
watching Buckley vs. Vidal
and wondering what all
the fuss was
about.

Neither
of them ever
left home
in a verbal
sense.

Their parent's basements
were still full of them
and all their dirty
socks.

Bayou Betty Finds Her Place in the Throaty Stomach Acid Amalgam

She drove around the south
in a camper
like it was the 1960s.

Thinking the best of everyone.
Taking in a street kid named "Nasty,"
then being surprised when he
stole from her.

Last I heard from her
she had taken a bar job
down along Bourbon.

Wiping puke
off the toilets
at 5:30 in the
morning.

New Orleans was her new home.
She was settling down.
Selling the camper.

To anyone not named "Nasty"
I would imagine.

The Receptionist

picked up phones
and put them
down

like a veterinarian
with a handful of sick
animals

and when the printer
was out of paper
she fixed that
too…

a real trouble
shooter.

Partial Eclipse

Moon board – a place to stand to view the partial eclipse
shoulder to shoulder with absent armies
children seated on the nape of their elders like
pointing wide-eyed scarves
and the women share recipes, but not in this moment
the fidgeting of fingers and nervous laughter
droplets of sweat though it is evening
vocal chords and exertion, thought of postcard
Stonehenge pasted to the fridge
ballyhoo and twisted knickers in a pinch
wooden slats underfoot that sag from the weight
like the faces of the elderly
a reverse rainbow of modern engineering which
threatens to collapse at any moment,
but does not,
and the festive sky is late
and it is past the children's bedtimes
but everyone waits,
not wanting to miss anything else.

Bundle Up

I had no idea that walls wore coats,
I say,
it that the second
or third?

I'm ignoring you,
she says
sliding the brush down the wall
in long confident strokes.

I dip my fingers in the paint can
and wipe it down my face.

Look at my war paint,
I puff out my naked chest,
too bad there is only
peace.

Too bad, she says.

I thought you were ignoring me.

I am,
she says.

Those overalls make you look fat,
I grin.

Now she needs her
war paint.

Falling Out of Bed
like the Last Days of
Saigon

This writing thing is a war really.
I have scars and the computer screen
has scars and no one looks like they
did before.

If you hunted down old yearbook photos
they may as well be someone else
entirely.

The growths and blood and baldness
and bloating
like a hot air balloon rendition
of yourself.

That has died a thousand deaths
and somehow felt each of them
thrice over.

Falling out of bed
like the last days of
Saigon.

Spitting up thick chunky yellow things
from the nasal passages
and throat.

Worshipping the chipmunk
because it is small enough to
forget about itself when
it needs to.

Besties

Their first place together
was this tiny basement in Letitia Heights
with a curtain divider
and I kept thinking, they won't be best friends
for long, just imagine when the other brings a man home from the ba
drunk and throwing her legs in the air and screaming
bloody murder when the other has to work in the morning;
they were both in the school choir so you know they had pipes,
and the kitchen was a kettle with a sink,
I gave them a month.

After three weeks,
they went their separate
ways.

One moved in with a man
she had met at the bar.

The other moved back home,
then to a new city
entirely.

What happened to the curtain divider
is anyone's guess.

Split Personalities, in a Physical Sense

The child in the street
picks up the grenade
and laughs.

Then it is blown apart
so the war against tyranny
can continue.

27lbs in 4 Weeks

The Goodyear blimp sails overhead
and I think of weight loss,
of the odd impulse to lose more
of your mortal self all the time,
then turn around and fear death
like your very own non-existence.

Isn't death the ultimate end game?
Of weight loss, and everything
else?

The bones picked clean by the waiting worms.
You are never more thin then when you are skeletonized.

And someone wins the sporting event on the television
and some else loses
and everything down to the jock straps
is sponsored.

The Goodyear blimp sailing away.
I imagine what stomach crunches would
feel like during a Bar Mitzvah.

Tearing fabric from the
couch cushions
like breaking families
apart.

The Wailing Wall
is the ultimate
whiner.

A Woman of Race

We were drunk enough for truth
and he asked me if I had ever been
with a woman of race
and I told him that the marathon runners
never did it for me because even sharing
a cup of coffee would take four hours
and life is short

and that the sprinters were in such a hurry
to everything
that they were more like men
working towards the finish line
when they could have been women
all along

and that the hurdlers just confounded me,
the same way people climb a mountain
to just say they almost ran
out of oxygen;

running errands is okay,
I do that too.

To fill the fridge,
and sometimes the
soul.

Art House

There is a Monet print
at the top of the
stairs.

A seascape
of which he is quite famous
for.

The pinks bring it all together
like so many of his
offerings.

Capturing the light.

Colouring each clumsy drunken
stumble up the
stairs.

And there is beauty there,
not at all like two abused animals
glued together
chewing off each other's faces
in a panic.

Or the hourly stretchmark woman who sits on top of you
like a headstone.

I adore that painting,
my simple print of it because I am a poor man
playing at being rich.

Smiling
when all the odds
demand you do

something
else.

Sofia

She writes from Sofia, Bulgaria
to tell me I "rattle her cage"
and I ask her how it is that an entire
city of women can live in a city
named after another woman
and no one gets catty.

The ones I have known will go off on you
at the simple mention of a
past dalliance.

Keying your car
and blaming mid-east
terrorism.

She laughs
and offers that perhaps
I do not know the
right women.

The assumption being, of course,
that she is the right woman
and I have just never been to Bulgaria.

Well the latter is true enough,
I have never been to Bulgaria.

It could be a beautiful country.
And she could be a wonderful lady.

But the cost of finding out is too much to bear.
And there are many ladies much closer to home.
Some with their own jobs and cars.

Basement Apartment

She always thought someone would rape her
because she lived alone in a basement apartment –
easy access, and all that –
and I told her there were already enough people
that couldn't sleep at night
without all the others just making things up
as they went along.

And that seemed to make her feel better.
Her young child in the next room up every few hours
for a feeding.

But she seemed disappointed in some way.
Like she took offence.
That the apparent lack of rapists
was a commentary on her
fading looks.

The last time I was over at her place
I was unscrewing a large oak wall unit
from the wall.

The dust that came off that thing.
It must have been half as old as Babylon.

And the way I drank too much
and drove most the way home
with the parking brake on.

Slowing for a dead deer in the road
that would now have maggots
for eyes.

Zebra Mussels

He goes to the gym
and there is not a zebra mussel
in site.

His long dead fisherman of a father
wildly disappointed
if the dead could be such
things.

That is how the living often imagine them;
wildly disappointed.

That his son moved to the city.
That you did not say what you wanted to say.
Have not made more of yourself.

These are hang ups of the living.
The dead have no hang ups.

Just a box or an urn
or a pyre
in ancient
times.

Ramen

She shovels ramen noodles
into her mouth
as though it may be snowing
somewhere.

In some distant white locale
where consecutive pods of sperm whales
sing their horny wet spouting
blubber children into one another.

And the cars in the street
jockey for position.

Signalling and honking
and changing lanes
and stopping.

It's like a horse race
that no one ever
bets on.

The glove compartment
full of maps to
nowhere.

And a single battery powered
flashlight in case the Dark Ages
ever return.

I am sleeping on the couch
because I am a guest,

beside a window cracked for air
and an empty upturned
fishbowl.

Following each line of hardwood
across the floor
back to
tree.

Punctured Lungs & Cryostasis

Ever notice how flip phones look like mob informants
you put to your ear?
The crassness of stand-up comedians never sitting well
with club owners?
It's a lot of sitting and standing, isn't it?
Punctured lungs and cryostasis.
Indian rope tricks in a bind.
Mountains high as speed freaks in an ecological sense...
I love my mind, the way it works and then doesn't work,
the circuit board taken out like witness testimony
so comfortable shoes can walk.
The atom split like the crack of your ass.
The collusion of mass circle jerks.
Solar flares just haemorrhoids for the celestial
appetite –
talk of space colonies over college radio
frat house sex and tuition hikes;
heavy breathing like a wind tunnel
with nice legs.

I want to join the army.
Not your army, but
mine.

An invasion of privacy planned for the spring.
When the weather is nicer, and some of the
ladies too.

Breasts Are Not a Sexual Thing

forget:

Jane Mansfield
Marilyn Monroe
Jean Harlow
Bette Davis
Mae West
Ginger Rogers
Grace Kelly
Marlene Dietrich
Veronica Lake
Lana Turner…

Yeah right!

Dish Hogs

The best thing about being a dish hog
in the city
is that no one else
wants to know
"the pork."

Or how you got there
in popular speak,
so you can go three or four weeks
before anyone talks to you.

And when they do, it is always
about drugs and dealers
and if you want the connections
or have better connections
than them.

At a certain point
they won't stop talking,
so that you start thinking them
a fink for the feds or the prosecution
or both.

Lose the War, Win the Fight

To write enough poems
and sell enough
hardware

to be locked up
in some Japanese luxury hotel

with an open bar
and a security detail all descended from
16th century shoguns

and an infinity pool on the roof
because god can fuck himself with
the sharp end of hubris
at three in the
morning,

where the environment is strangely sterile
and the hallway is full of flowers
that never die

and every moment
is a moment of
silence

unless you are in
the lobby,

then it is
loud.

Big Winner

The casino is there
the same way the child kidnapper
is there

but you are all grown up now
in a general musculature
sense

which makes hunting season legal

that tuneful sound for the gambling ear
oxygen pumped in so you can get high
on the moment

the bodies
dangling in the bathrooms
bagged and rushed out

so as not to kill
the buzz.

She Had a Nice Smile

They said she was a whore,
kneeled behind dumpsters
for the company glue,
but I could not find one of them
that held up under scrutiny.

It was like life on other planets.
No one had ever been there,
but they all believed it.

All their stories anorexic thin.
Returning to the Men's shelter
hallway up Princess
before ten o'clock lice
check.

Most with families that refused to see them.
The courts cutting in like a more handsome
and resourceful version of yourself.

And I made sure to never meet her
because there is no romance
in the street.

The peelers peel like potato skins
and the others do
more.

All I knew for sure
was that she lived on and off
with some black dude named DeShone

on the wrong side of Concession
who beat her
when his mother was not home,
and that she still had
most of her
teeth.

True Story

The Americans wanted into the Cuban embassy
in Montreal
so the RCMP set it on fire.
Then they were brought in to investigate
the cause of the fire
and found a treasure trove of paperwork
which they sent off to
the Americans.

No one knows how helpful it was.
But it really happened.

And even if you were to tell someone
they would not care or believe
you.

We are the good guys
forever.

Weak Play

I have cried over swirling dead goldfish
flushed back into the drinking water.

What kind of man does that?

Belly up with dark spots from when the oxygen
finally ran out.

Myself seated over the lip of the tub,
weeping in absentia.

More for me and the loss
than for anything
else.

A weak play, I kept telling myself,
if there is a feebler man alive
you have not met him.

Then I would run a bath
and sit in it until the water ran cold,
pretending to be a goldfish.

Dressing afterwards
at the foot of the bed
with all the care of a mortuary
full of stiffs.

Lunar Eclipse

The fact
that the ancients
felt the need
to build monuments
to the sun
being blocked out
for a moment
in time

does little to reassure me
about all the idiots
out on the street
right now

with their children propped up
on their shoulders
pointing toward the
sky

trying to forget
that there is work in the morning
and that they are expected
to be there.

The Queen's Speech

She gets mad at me when I laugh at the royals.

*You know they were planning to move the queen
in case of invasion,*
she says,
*that's how close it came.
London was bombed each night.*

*And they knocked off Di because ole Charlie
was schlepping a commoner.
That can't sit well with you first rate
palace floozies.*

She does not deny they Di was killed by the royals,
but she still tunes in for the Queen's speech
each Christmas.

A terrible balancing act, I must imagine.
If you are into that whole gold-encrusted
sort of thing.

She watches it with her aunt.
Both Scottish nationals.

Then she comes home
and makes me watch
it.

To which I always ask:
is the old bag not dead yet?

Before walking off.

Sashimi Thin

You don't expect to find all these clothing hangers
in the men's bathroom.

She has told me about the many stacks
in the women's bathroom,
how they cough each time
even though you know what
they are doing.

And she does not seem surprised
that the men have finally gotten in
on the hustle.

There were so many hangers I had to count them,
I tell her.

The guy who walked out before me
still had the tags attached.

And we are sitting in the mall food court.
She orders something half-healthy
and I order something smothered
in gravy.

Before we visit the ring shops
and find out we have obscenely large
fingers.

Like Godzilla walking into pinball Tokyo
on a dare,
looking for fresh
sushi.

Full Uniform

It was after the soccer game.
We had lost 5-3.
I took it personally even though
such things are a team sport.

And I was in full uniform
as we climbed the steep hill
up to St. Mary's Church.
My father and brother and I.
My cleats making me sound like a
horse drawn carriage over tourist
dollar cobblestone.

And once inside the church I felt better.
Like a soccer game didn't matter anymore.
And my father had always made fun of god
and the church, but we always had to come
see Father Ted.

And I remember looking up at that intoxicating
shimmering blue colour of the large stained glass windows
that made me feel so wonderfully small.

As my brother played hide and seek
with himself in the pews
and Father Ted talked with
my own father by the
pulpit.

The Real Thing

I had fallen into the arms of higher learning
in a different city
because anyone too smart for everything
tends to fall into anything

and he felt that he had been
left behind

to stock the graveyard shelves alone
with a cat that had gotten into a fight
with something it shouldn't have
and lost

and when I returned
the cat was locked in the bedroom
dying of its wounds by the hour

while he got out his credit card
so we could cut lines of coke
over a nine inch nails cd
and snort them together
for one last time

as friends

while the dealers sat on a black futon
behind us
still counting the
money.

Tiny Marathon Runners with Flush Numbered Bellybuttons

I get on the bus
and the driver seems
to hate me.

As though I may have rustled his cattle
in a past life
and my mere presence is
ruining his day.

I only stumble a few steps
before falling between some sweaty
fat black woman lost to her horoscopes
and a kid with drumsticks for hands
meeting his knees halfway.

It is the sound of an agitated virginity.
Send a professional girl or two his way
and he's as tranquil as warm milk.

Lazy in both eyes
as we all should
be.

But I catch the driver in the mirror.
Mean mugging me with a mouthful
of quivering snarls.

And the sweat runs down his cheeks.
Tiny marathon runners with flush
numbered bellybuttons.

Half of starving Africa
looking to defect with the next
Olympics.

And when I ring the bell,
the driver seems as though
he doesn't want to let
me off.

I thank him anyways
and walk over sidewalks
put there by the city.

Past professional buildings
devoid of professionals

and the employment building
where no one can get
a job

with a ball of tissues
in my left pant
pocket

waiting for my sinuses
to act up.

Bathroom Break

Back from the bathroom
you feel lighter,
the bladder voided,
the bowels evacuated
like an office tower bomb threat
floor-by-floor,
and you do a little dance
like Christopher Walken
in every crappy movie
he has ever made.

I much prefer Christopher Walken the philosopher:

I think that weddings have probably been crashed since the beginning of time. Cavemen crashed them. You go to meet girls. It makes sense.

Something so stupid and simple and true that Marcus Aurelius
could never have fumbled upon it
simply because fumbling was below him.

That is the problem with always looking skyward.
You miss the tumult of the dirt.

The worms
and the tilling of
soil.

Myself
just back from the
bathroom.

Fluency Test

The bilingual people made him take
a fluency test
because speaking in tongues
was no longer the work of the devil
and was now mandatory for
any government job,
the exorcist replaced by the chemist,
handing you a bottle to piss in
so they could determine if you were
a fiend,

and I guess his sample came
back clean

because he works for the government
now

with a security clearance
and everything,
like needing a secret third nipple
to walk into your own shirt
closet.

Life

We play the game of life
and I end up with a car full of kids
I can't pay for.

Why would anyone play this bloody game,
I ask?

I told you to get a college education,
she answers.

How would that help with all the kids?,
I ask,
if I have any more, I'll be running a polygamy commune
out of the backwoods of snowy Utah.

Don't be a sore loser,
she says
like someone who
never loses.

I don't need this shit right now,
I say.

We are rained in.
She has called in sick.

Not because she is sick,
but because something about
the general mechanism of
the 40 hour week
is taxing.

Prostitutes leaning into cars
at right angles.

The husbandry of crack houses.

After Ketchup
and grilled cheese
sandwiches.

The curtains pulled over
like the sun going
out.

We climb under the blankets
and threaten to tickle
one another.

She wearing my undershorts
for a change.

Holdout

He decided to
holdout
because everyone
else
was getting
paid

even though
he was a running back
on the wrong side
of thirty

and there were injuries

and a few teams brought him in
for a physical,
nothing serious,
really just to threaten their own
backs into re-signing
for less

and he fired his agent
and decided to represent
himself

which went as well
as it always does
when no one is standing
behind you

and you have to do everything
yourself.

PTSD

There was a support group
that met each day
but they didn't understand
anything.

And those feel good proponents of patting a dog
on the head for a half hour each week
to make up for the horror of
everything else.

And PFC Gibson sat in his ward room
with the privacy curtain
pulled over.

Waiting for the nurse
to bring his nightly
trazodone.

Sporting Goods

She took a job in the Canadian Tire
sporting goods section
even though she knew nothing
about sports.

Because the manager at the Harvey's
would not hire her to flip burgers.

And sometimes in the evenings
we would sit at the Burger King
across from the box store
where I was lucky enough to stock
fruits and vegetables
imported from god knows where,
so we could make rent
and splurge,

asking for mayonnaise
with our fries

like no one had
it better.

Vampires with Hate for Horse Blinders

There is nothing dumber
in this world than a man who hates women
simply for being women

or a woman who hates men
for being men.

But that won't stop them.
They want their blood.
Vampires with hate for horse blinders.
Gathering in the streets to protest the mere existence
of the other.

As we all try to work and eat
and sleep and survive.

Often dependant on one another,
as much as the raving loonies may not
like it.

Regardless of what is taught in the universities
these days.

We are stuck here together
for better or worse.

Get over it.

The Artist and The General

my eyes are gorged
with the sting of tiredness,
of overturned laundry baskets
in fixated alcoves,
snakeskin boots on arid coffee tables,
a pooling along the base
where a single beer can has come
to rest,
seeping under glass,
and there are two voices in my head:
the artist and the general,
the general says: be done with it
streamline, trim the fat
onward ho!

while the artist drinks too much
grows silly with wonder, keeps meddling
fidgeting away like a spider
under rocks,

and with no one steering the train
everyone is steering the train,
laying down on the tracks,
but never sleeping…

if I could have an acetate pressed
like a panini sandwich
I would slither into my own restless
ears at 34 rpms,
getting caught up in the wax

while the grass drives off in a car
made of lawnmowers

and my sinuses fill with mucus
like a hall of concertgoers.

Did you hear the one…

about the man who was woken
from cryostasis after 700 years
as a popsicle
and thawed out so that he could give
a reading at the university,
and how the audience could
not stop laughing telekinetically
as the old timer asked where
all the books had gone?

Expiration Date

You
are
here
for
a
time

and
then

you
are
not,

why
all
this
fuss

over
expired

coupons?

Consumption

Arterial blood
you get to know the colour,
Keats on his deathbed
after his time in medical school;
it is not enough to be fucked,
they want you to know it as well.
Like an aging carriage horse passing
the glue factory.
Young lovers in back holding hands,
enjoying the sound of clopping hooves
over cobblestone,
the scenery…

I never learned to play the guitar.
I tried and failed.
Then I sold the guitar as others
sell their time.

Now I sit drooping halfway down
into the couch cushions.

On a sharp angle like they teach in geometry.

Squishing bugs into the wall that try
to keep me company.

Pickled Requiem

everybody said it

nobody meant
it

taking care of business

hits and misses
hers and his

ain't got no Eldorado
in this fight

blanching distant coral

shipwrecks pulled up
like wood suspenders

nobody said it

everybody meant
it

too late now

the lights gone
out.

Centenarian

100 window ledges of dead flydom
100 sitting chairs as though there are any other kind
count backwards from 100 until you are rutabaga red in the face
100 Roman legions tossing spears into the afterlife
100 silly miracles from a rock face steep as runaway doorstops
100 days with no money down
100 stash houses in a 20 block radius
92 could be 100 if it had just tried harder
100 planes drop out of the sky each year like winged confetti
100 virgins sounds like way too much work
100 calories or less
100 cigarettes, and only one mouth to smoke them
100 nuts for every bolt at the madhouse
100 duplexes before you can finally urinate on your own
100 page novellas selling half as well as keychains
100 hours of free streaming in refinished basements
100 roses will set you back
I could count to 100 by the time I was in 3rd grade according to my report cards
100 proof breath
100 comets pass the earth every hour like extracurricular kidney stones
page 100 of For Whom The Bells Toll starts with the word "You"
100 barf bags caught up in an air sickness ring
100 necks for the albatross to frequent, and it finds yours
100 nunneries and still no god
100 arguments later there is no consensus

she has left you 100 times
and returned 100 times
100 degree heat where sunscreen comes into its own
100   1 hundred   one hundred…

that is my lucky
number.

Late Night Feedings

He stood over the company paper shredder.

Not as though it was wrong,
but rather his job.

His solemn duty to break paper down
to mulch.
Paper that had once been trees
just showing off.

The hubris of the stupid green rainforest
finally giving way.

Returning to the cold dank earth
of everything.

And there were annual bonuses
to consider.

The promise of promotion
like growing three inches taller
in a single calendar year
of late adulthood.

Expense accounts
on the company
dime.

Personal secretaries under the desk
that could always pretend to be looking
for your pencil.
And there were other things to consider as well.

Like the things they had on you
from day one
so that you would keep doing more things
for them that they could have
on you.

Things build on one another
like stacking palates.

And no one could remember a time
when they had not been had.

It may have started with Santa Claus.
Being taken like that year
after year.

Tricked into believing.
Like watching a magic show cut someone in half
who then smiles at you to great
applause.

And so he found himself standing in the dark.
Over the company paper shredder
after hours.

Taking everything down the back service elevator
to a private removal company
that had a fleet of trucks
all around the city

working around the clock

that dealt in such
delicate matters.

Exit Strategy

To become entangled in a volleyball net,
there are far greater impediments than that.

Take if you will, the car that won't start.
Public transit to work as though you are seventeen
all over again.

Or worse still, walking.

Manning the phones at the telemarketers.
Cheating half-demented old pensioners
out of their livelihood
25 hours a week
for $5.75/hr.

The script in front of you.
Targeting them like rooftop snipers
in a war no one even knows
they are fighting.

Mortality ensures there is only one
exit strategy for us all.

Beyond all the bloom and bluster.

Flowers that never find beauty
fail at everything else.

Swimmers without Goggles

She has just finished swallowing
the best of you down
and there is money on the table
like ladies in waiting
as she retreats to the bathroom
with her purse full
of mouthwash

to check her phone
and make sure the next date
a few blocks away
under the name: Hector
is still a go.

Hell, with a Broken Radio

I pull up to the pumps
and hop out with the company gas card,
trying to wipe old welder burns off my pants.

Not that I am a welder,
but rather the 19 year old sheet metal grunt
brought in to hold the joints in place, then load the truck
and drive it through hell with a broken radio
for $10/hr.

And the filling station is at the end of the street
in a whole different city I lived in only
three years previous.

And I think about driving by the old house,
but decide that would be weird.

It is not until I go in to pay
that I realize the gas card is not accepted
at this particular station.

They are the competition
are seem rather certain about
that fact.

So I pull out my bank card
and pray I have the $20 in there
to cover it.

The young Indian kid behind the glass
is as surprised as I am when it comes back cleared

and he hands me my receipt.

Then it is back up into the truck
for the hour and ten minute drive
back south to the city.

On Fighting

I have no problem with fighting
as long as the endeavour is fair:
no weapons or swarming gangs
or any of that nonsense.

And the fight should be consensual
like sex,
anything else is just beating up
on someone.

Outside of that,
go to town.

And if you happen to be in a city,
go larger than
that.

Long Lines at the Grocers so Cars can be Loaded full as Sniper's Rifles

I am not here to be aesthetically pleasing
I am not here to be politically correct
I am not here long
I am not here completely

not here nor
there

I am three consecutive knots in a rancher's
brown taut rope

I am bevelled wood and glaucoma

I am the medal of honour
in a blue felt case
sentimentality opened
on special occasions

I am the North Sea and the South Sea
and every fish on ice

my cold dead eyeballs peering up into
hard light

fins cut away from the working whole
like piloting a rudderless boat

long lines at the grocers
so cars can be loaded full as

sniper's rifles

and aimed at popular
intersections

the roads painted with lines
so as not to look like either roads
or lines…

I can see it
I am Hubble
I am a telescope lodged deep into the fiery
Promethean skull of curiosity

high resolution
as they say in the
business

government spooks under the bed
molesting your box spring
into general compliance

and there is a reason torture is illegal:
it works

the same way no one will allow you
to run naked down the avenues
citing an acute absence of clothing

six lanes of onlookers all honking their horns
like the Ford Motor Company
on ecstasy

as you wave in the wind like

a long drooping flag

anthems sung
like Christmas carols
out of season

one country from another
just shoes on the opposite
foot

I am their laces
I am frayed and in need
of replacement

I am the green electrical box humming
of expensive song

walking into a store
my life is divided into aisles

the needs surrounded by the wants
like any good hustle

a young attractive cashier without
a single brain in her head

smiling at you
the way a billboard along the freeway
commands your attention

cows in distant fields
sitting for the rain

milking the system if you can swing it

disability is a great word,
isn't it?

like a grant system for the impoverished
and uneducated

playing your father's entire record collection backwards
looking for Satan

impregnation
and schoolyard tether ball
losing tether

the nuclear family wound tight
as Swiss clocks

grandfathers placed in prominent handcrafted corners
so the dead do not seem so old
or far away or forgotten

aeroplanes full of peanut allergies
and flatulence

window seats
so the gathering watery nimbus clouds
can fall prey to hubris

pot dispensaries
on every block

everything legal
like your first cousin is finally
in play

the human genome
a pack of sesame seeds spit out
of the aching flirty birdfeeder
of too much to eat

and I am an abridged novel
on four set cd

Zen Buddhism
and beach front
property –

see you in the fall
when preachy Johnny Milton
makes the most
of coloured
leaves

to the
ground.

Major Depressive Disorder

1000 lbs limbs,
you know
them.

Unable to move
or function.

Even with the medications.

Fourteen hours in bed
and you wake up exhausted.

Shower if it is a good day.
It is debilitating.

No employer wants a truant.
And so you drink when you can.
To fill the hours.
So as not to think or feel.

I am sorry to be so depressive all the time,
but my previous humour escapes me.

It is not that I don't want it back.
Oh to laugh and laugh
and laugh…

The ribbed sides hurting again.

Like a mountain
just before an avalanche.

Work Clothes

I am steeping tea
because I am allergic to coffee.

Caffeine to be exact.
Sure I could drink decaf,
but that would be like paying
for a hooker that "doesn't do that."

And the radiator is broken.
And the building superintendent
died seven years ago.

We all just figure it out now
as we go.

Connected by little more than the
overpowering aroma of our clumsy work clothes
existence.

Ryan Quinn Flanagan is a Canadian-born author residing in Elliot Lake, Ontario, Canada with his wife and many bears that rifle through his garbage. His work can be found both in print and online in such places as: Evergreen Review, The New York Quarterly, In Between Hangovers, Red Fez, and the Oklahoma Review. His personal website is: ryanquinnflanagan.yolasite.com.

Some of these poems have previously appeared: *Alien Buddha Press, Anti-Heroin Chic, Duane's PoeTree, Five 2 One Magazine, FLULAND, Horror Sleaze Trash, In Between Hangovers, Mad Swirl, Midnight Lane Boutique, Outsider Poetry, Pski's Porch, Setu, The Australia Times Poetry Magazine, The Beautiful Space, VerseWrights, Walking Is Still Honest, Your One Phone Call.*

Pski's Porch Publishing was formed July 2012, to make books for people who like people who like books.
We hope we have some small successes.
www.pskisporch.com.

323 East Avenue
Lockport, NY 14094
www.pskisporch.com

www.ingramcontent.com/pod-product-compliance
Lightning Source LLC
Chambersburg PA
CBHW071217090426
42736CB00014B/2862